50p.

Early skills

The illustrations and activities in this book are planned to develop pre-reading and pre-maths skills: matching, recognising differences, counting and concentrating on detail.

Nature

Most children love talking about animals. It's fun to imitate the way animals move and the noises they make – this is a wonderful opportunity for talking and laughing. You can wonder together what it feels like to be a bird, a tree, a butterfly – or even a ladybird.

Picture stories

Talking about picture stories helps children to understand that things happen in an order, with a 'before' and an 'after'. Tell the story yourself first, using the pictures to help. Soon your child will want to join in and experience the thrill of behaving like a real reader.

Other Talkabout Books to help you and your child

- animals
- home
- shopping
- baby
- starting school
- bedtime
- going into hospital

Geraldine Taylor is a national broadcaster, writer and authority on involving parents in their children's education. She contributes on this subject regularly to magazines for parents.

Working with schools in Avon, Geraldine helps parents and teachers to act in partnership to benefit children's learning confidence and family happiness.

Contents

British Library Cataloguing in Publication Data

Taylor, Geraldine
My first big talkabout.
1. English language
I. Title II. Edwards, Gunvor
428.6

ISBN 0-7214-7543-4

First edition

Published by Ladybird Books Ltd Loughborough Leicestershire UK Ladybird Books Inc Auburn Maine 04210 USA

Printed in England (7)

My First
Big Talkabout

by GERALDINE TAYLOR
illustrated by GUNVOR EDWARDS

Ladybird Books

Hello!

What's your name?

What colour is your hair?

What is your favourite colour?

What colour are your eyes?

Can you hop on one leg?

Can you clap your hands?

Can you jump up and down?

Can you run round in a circle?

Lots of homes

Where do you live?

Good morning!

It's time to get up!

Breakfast time

What do you like to eat?

Can you sing this song?

Chorus *(to follow each verse)*

Here we go round the mulberry bush,
The mulberry bush, the mulberry bush,
Here we go round the mulberry bush,
On a cold and frosty morning.

This is the way we wash our hands,
Wash our hands, wash our hands,
This is the way we wash our hands,
On a cold and frosty morning.

This is the way we wash our face,
Wash our face, wash our face,
This is the way we wash our face,
On a cold and frosty morning.

This is the way we comb our hair,
Comb our hair, comb our hair,
This is the way we comb our hair,
On a cold and frosty morning.

This is the way we tie our shoes,
Tie our shoes, tie our shoes,
This is the way we tie our shoes,
On a cold and frosty morning.

This is the way we go to school,
Go to school, go to school,
This is the way we go to school,
On a cold and frosty morning.

Is it cold today?

Do you like it when...

...it's raining?

...it's hot?

...it's windy?

...it's cold?

Which do you like best?

Going out

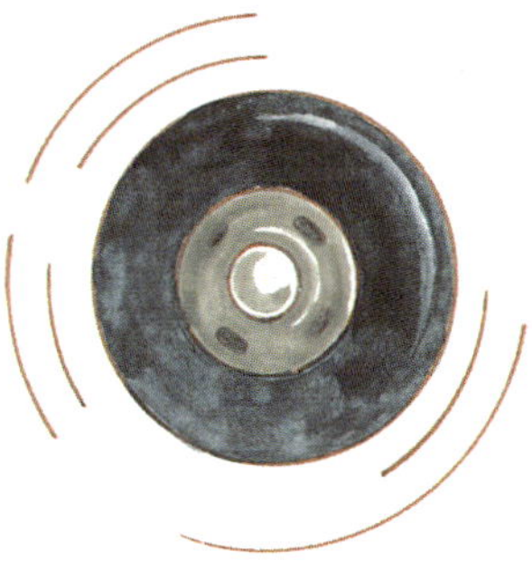

The wheels on the bus go round and round,
Round and round, round and round.
The wheels on the bus go round and round,
All day long.

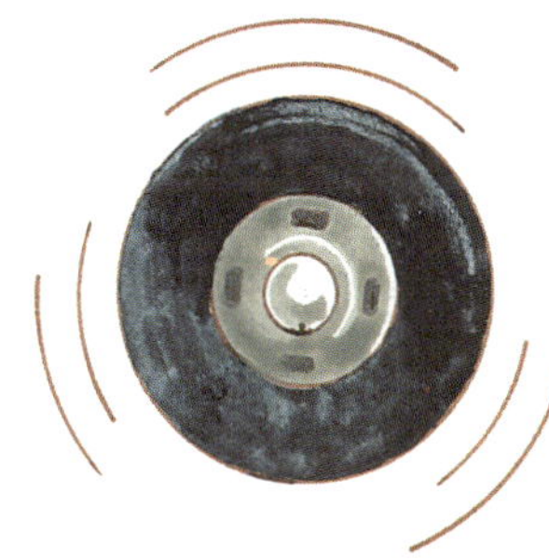

The horn on the bus goes peep, peep, peep,
Peep, peep, peep, peep, peep, peep.
The horn on the bus goes peep, peep, peep,
All day long.

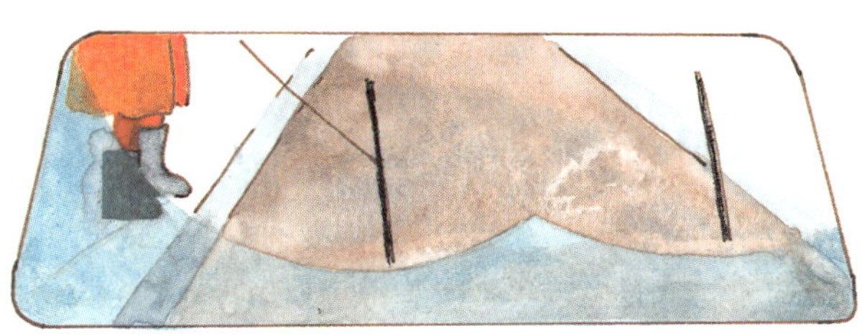

The wipers on the bus go swish, swish, swish,
Swish, swish, swish, swish, swish, swish.
The wipers on the bus go swish, swish, swish,
All day long.

The people on the bus bounce up and down,
Up and down, up and down.
The people on the bus bounce up and down,
All day long.

shopping

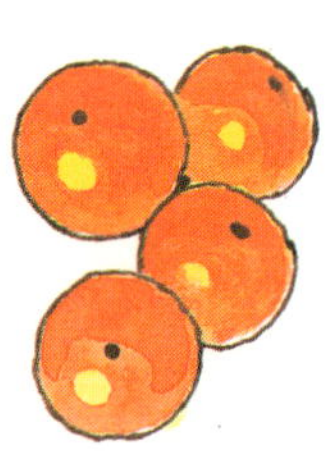

Do you know these rhymes about shopping?

Smiling girls, rosy boys,
Come and buy my little toys.
Monkeys made of gingerbread
And sugar horses painted red.

Cobbler, cobbler, mend my shoe,
Get it done by half past two.
My toe is peeping through,
Cobbler, cobbler, mend my shoe.

One day I went to Darlington,
That pretty little town,
And there I bought a petticoat,
A cloak, and a gown.

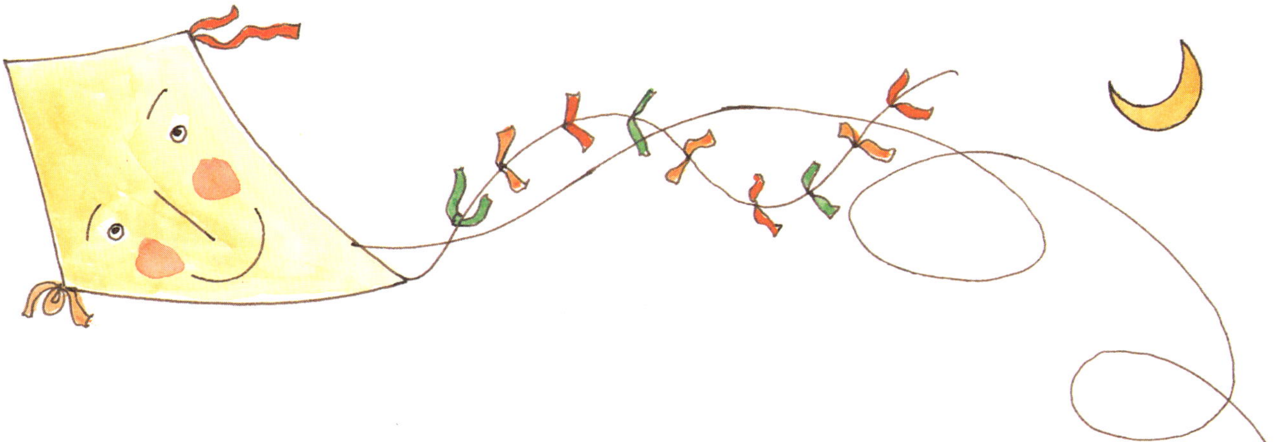

What shall you buy?
A kite that will fly
Up to the moon
All through the sky.

Here's a large one for the lady,
Here's a small one for the baby,
Come buy, my pretty lady
Come buy me a broom.

To market, to market,
To buy a plum bun.
Home again, home again,
Market is done.

Helping at home

It's raining!

I hear thunder,
I hear thunder;
Hark don't you?
Hark don't you?
Pitter-patter raindrops,
Pitter-patter raindrops,
I'm wet through,
So are you!

Here comes the sun!

I see blue skies,
I see blue skies,
Way up high,
Way up high,
Hurry up the sunshine,
Hurry up the sunshine,
I'll soon dry,
I'll soon dry.

Picture storytime

Let's play!

Do you know what happens...

...at the doctor's?

...at the dentist's?

...at the optician's?

Miss Polly had a dolly
Who was sick, sick, sick.
So she 'phoned for the doctor
To be quick, quick, quick.

The doctor came
With his bag and his hat,
And he rapped at the door
With a rat-tat-tat.

He looked at the dolly
And he shook his head.
Then he said, ''Miss Polly,
Put her straight to bed.''

He wrote on a paper
For a pill, pill, pill;
''I'll be back in the morning
With my bill, bill, bill.''

Farmyard animals

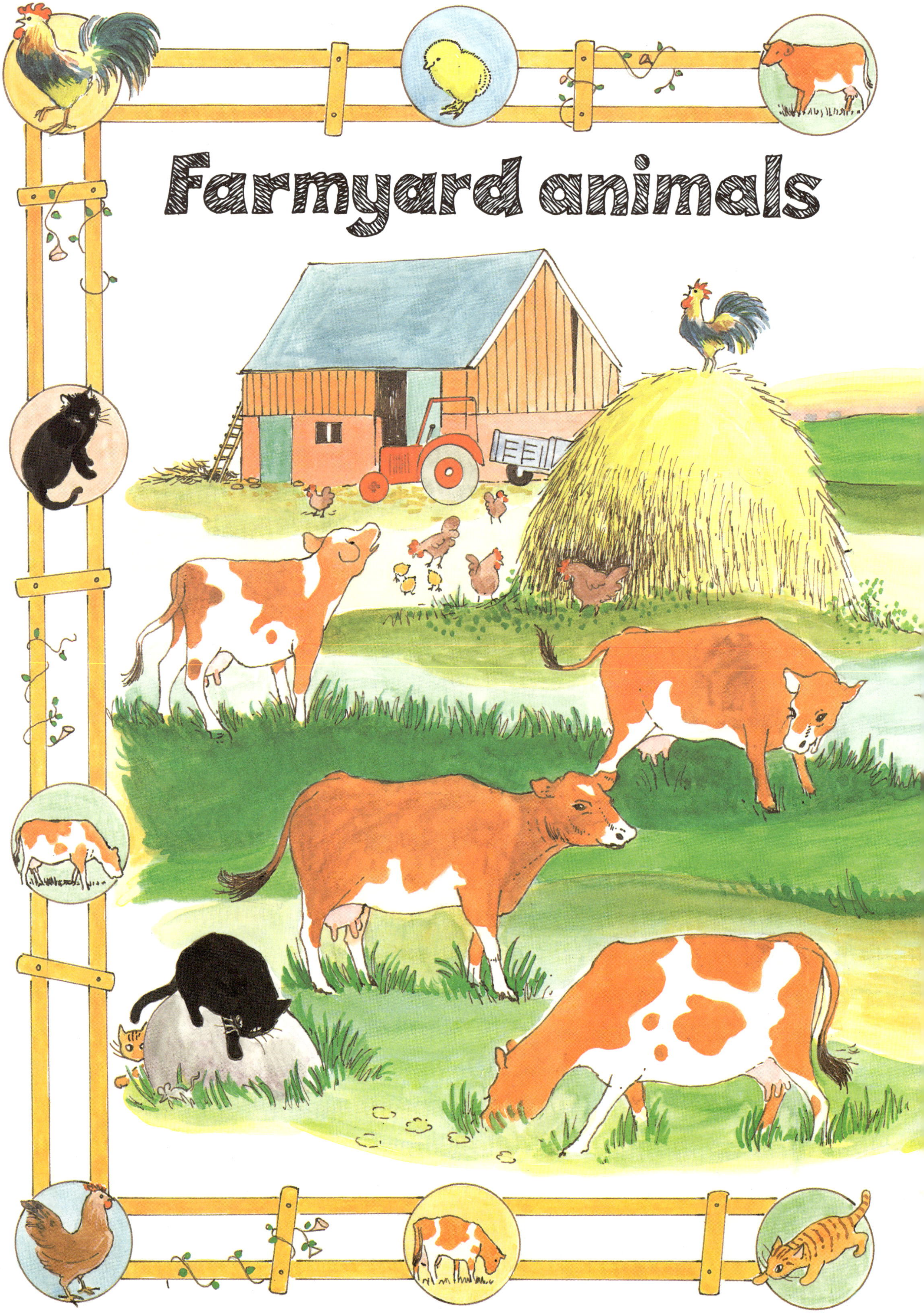

Can you count these?

1 2 3 4 5

Can you find them again?

Animal rhymes

An elephant walks like this and that,
He's terribly tall and terribly fat.
He has no fingers,
He has no toes,
But goodness gracious, what a nose!

The tortoise can't go out to play
Or sell his house or rent it;
For when he moves,
His house moves too
And nothing can prevent it.

Higgledy Piggledy, my black hen,
She lays eggs for gentlemen;
Sometimes nine and sometimes ten,
Higgledy Piggledy, my black hen.

Would you like one
of these as a pet?

Have you heard these?

Have you smelt these?

Have you touched these?

Have you tasted these?

How many of these have you seen?

Are your favourite things here?

Happy Birthday

How old are you?

Have you done any of these things today?

What do you like to pretend to be?

Time for a story

9
10
11
12
13
14
15
16

Bedtime!

Good night!

Niddledy, noddley,
To and fro,
Tired and sleepy,
To bed we go.
Jump into bed,
Switch out the light,
Head on the pillow,
Shut your eyes tight.

See you in the morning!